Things That *Grab Your Heart* and Won't Let Go

Stories That Will Give You *Goose Bumps*

MAC ANDERSON

simple truths®
Your Destination For Inspiration
an imprint of Sourcebooks, Inc.

Editing by: Alice Patenaude

Photo Credits
Cover: NatalieShuttleworth/Getty Images
Internals: page 1, NatalieShuttleworth/Getty Images; page 4, ooyoo/iStock; page 6, javarman3/Thinkstock; page 8, Purestock/Thinkstock; pages 10–11, nataliafrei/Shutterstock; page 12, Max Topchii/Shutterstock; page 15, Deklofenak/Shutterstock; page 17, Levranii/Shutterstock; pages 18–19; marekuliasz/Thinkstock; page 20, Tommy Alsén/Thinkstock; page 22, Brian Frantz/Sourcebooks, Inc.; pages 24–25, crossstudio/Thinkstock; page 26, Suzanne Tucker/Shutterstock; pages 28–29, knape/iStock, leminuit/iStock; page 31, Vladimir Surkov/Thinkstock; page 32, 4FR/Getty Images; page 33, Monkey Business Images/Shutterstock; pages 34–35, stevecoleimages/iStock; page 36, Purestock/Thinkstock; page 38, hadynyah/iStock; pages 40–41, Davidenko Pavel/Thinkstock; page 42, Warren Goldswain/Shutterstock; page 43, Dina Uretski/Shutterstock; page 45, asife/Shutterstock; page 46, Deborah Pendell/Getty Images; page 48, A.KaZaK/Shutterstock; page 51, Kovnir Andrii/Shutterstock; pages 52–53, Karina Walton/Thinkstock; page 54, tirc83/Thinkstock; page 55, logoboom/iStock; page 57, Mordolff/iStock; pages 58–59, Phase4Studios/Shutterstock; page 61, Jupiterimages/Thinkstock; page 62, Ryan McVay/Thinkstock; pages 66–67, Dave King/Thinkstock; page 68, m. uptegrove/Shutterstock; pages 70–71, Dalibor Sevaljevic/Shutterstock; pages 73, LoloStock/Shutterstock; pages 74–75, Creatas/Thinkstock; page 76, John Giustina/Getty Images; page 78, Mike Watson Images/Thinkstock; pages 80–81, Sunny_baby/Shutterstock; page 83, rrrua/iStock; pages 84–85, Studio-Annika/Thinkstock; pages 86–87, Warren Goldswain/Shutterstock; page 88, Pete Saloutos/Thinkstock; page 90, Purestock/Thinkstock; page 93, Shelly Perry/Thinkstock; pages 94–95, Aleksandr Doodko/Shutterstock; page 96, Anna Bizoa/Thinkstock; page 98, marcovarro/Shutterstock; page 99, Inmacor/Getty Images; pages 100–101, gpointstudio/Shutterstock; page 102, Paul Bradbury/Getty Images; page 104, TommL/Thinkstock; pages 106–107, 36clicks/Thinkstock; page 109, peepo/Getty Images; pages 110–111, Troels Graugaard/Getty Images; page 112, Kondoros Éva Katalin/Getty Images; page 113, Smiltena/Shutterstock; page 114, Mehmet Dilsiz/Shutterstock; page 117, Kolett/Shutterstock; page 118, Tatyana Vyc/Shutterstock; pages 120–121, Inc/Shutterstock; page 122, Artens/Shutterstock; page 124, EpicStockMedia/Shutterstock; page 127, EpicStockMedia/Thinkstock; page 128, Erik de Graaf/Thinkstock; page 131, AVAVA/Thinkstock; page 133, Ingram Publishing/Thinkstock; pages 134–135, Massonstock/Thinkstock; page 136, Joye Ardyn Durham/Thinkstock; page 139, Florin Stana/Shutterstock; pages 140–141, WerksMedia/Thinkstock

Published by Simple Truths, an imprint of Sourcebooks, Inc.
P.O. Box 4410, Naperville, Illinois 60567-4410
(630) 961-3900
Fax: (630) 961-2168
www.sourcebooks.com

Printed and bound in China.
RRD 10 9 8 7 6 5 4 3

CONTENTS

INTRODUCTION

A few years ago, I wrote the book *The Power of Attitude*. I'm pleased to say it has done well, selling more than 250,000 copies. However, after writing it, I gave copies to friends and family, and almost without exception, I'd hear the same feedback: "Mac, I loved your book, but what I really loved was that beautiful poem 'The Dash' on page 26." And then, the same few words would come out of their mouths. "It gave me goose bumps!" And you know what? That's exactly what happened to me when I read "The Dash" for the first time. It bypassed my brain and went straight to my heart to create that emotional sensation we often call "goose bumps."

We started Simple Truths seven years ago, and we've been privileged to publish more than one hundred books, sharing beautiful stories and poems like "The Dash." And for me, anyway, the true test of a great story is this…when I've finished reading it, did it give me goose bumps?

That's what this beautiful book is all about…a collection of inspirational stories and poems that grabbed my heart and would not let go. I hope you enjoy them as much as I did!

All the best,

An attitude of gratitude

WHEN WE CHOOSE NOT TO FOCUS
ON WHAT IS MISSING FROM OUR LIVES BUT
ARE GRATEFUL FOR THE ABUNDANCE THAT'S PRESENT...
WE EXPERIENCE HEAVEN ON EARTH.

≈ *Sarah Ban Breathnach* ≈

A Hero for the Ages

A story by MAC ANDERSON

❋

We all face adversity in our lives. However, it's not the adversity but how we react to it that determines the joy and happiness in our lives. I want to share a story with you that more than five years later still gives me goose bumps.

The date was July 16, 2008. It was late in the afternoon and I was sitting in my hotel room in Louisville, Kentucky. I was scheduled to speak that evening to 1,500 school principals, but I was a little "down in the dumps." My travel schedule had been hectic and my exercise schedule had suffered.

My keynote presentation was scheduled for 7:00 p.m., but I had been invited to show up at 6:00 p.m. to see a performance they said I'd enjoy. Little did I know I was about to see something I would never forget.

They introduced the young musician. Welcome…Mr. Patrick Henry Hughes. He was rolled onto the stage in his wheelchair and began to play the piano. His fingers danced across the keys as he made beautiful music.

He then began to sing as he played, and it was even more beautiful. There was this aura about him that I really can't explain and the smile…his smile was magic!

About ten minutes into Patrick's performance, someone came on the stage and said, "I'd like to share a seven-minute video titled 'The Patrick Henry Hughes Story.'" And the lights went dim.

Patrick Henry Hughes was born with no eyes and a tightening of the joints that left him disabled for life. However, as a child, he was fitted with artificial eyes and placed in a wheelchair. Before his first birthday, he discovered the piano. His mom said, "I could hit any note on the piano, and within one or two tries, he'd get it." By his second birthday, he was playing requests ("You Are My Sunshine," "Twinkle Twinkle Little Star"). His father was ecstatic. "We might not play baseball, but we can play music together," he said.

At the time of his performance, Patrick was a junior at the University of Louisville. His father attended classes with him and Patrick earned nearly all As, with the exception of three Bs. He was also part of the 214-member marching band. You read it right…the marching band! He was a blind, wheelchair-bound trumpet player; he and his father did it together. They attended all the band practices and the halftime performances in front of thousands. His father rolled and rotated his son around the field to the cheers of Patrick's fans. In order to attend Patrick's classes and every band practice, his father worked graveyard shifts at UPS. Patrick said, "My dad's my hero."

But even more than his unbelievable musical talent, it was Patrick's "attitude of gratitude" that touched my soul. On stage between songs, he talked to the audience about his life and about how blessed he was. He said, "God made me blind and unable to walk. BIG DEAL! He gave me the ability…the musical gifts I have…the great opportunity to meet new people."

When his performance was over, Patrick and his father were on the stage together. The crowd rose to their feet and cheered for more than five minutes. It gave me chills!

My life was ready to meet Patrick Henry Hughes. I needed a hero and I found one for the ages.

Excerpted from the introduction of the Simple Truths book
Learning to Dance in the Rain: The Power of Gratitude by Mac Anderson

We tend to forget that happiness doesn't come as a result of getting something we don't have, but rather of RECOGNIZING and APPRECIATING what we do have.

≈ *Frederick Keonig* ≈

GRATITUDE

unlocks the fullness of life. It turns what we have into enough,
and more. It turns denial into acceptance, chaos to order, confusion
to clarity. It can turn a meal into a feast, a house into a home,
a stranger into a friend… Gratitude makes sense of our past,
brings peace for today, and creates a vision for tomorrow.

≈ *Melody Beattie* ≈

Time spent with loved ones

OUR GREATEST DANGER IN LIFE IS IN PERMITTING THE
URGENT THINGS TO CROWD OUT THE IMPORTANT.

≈ *Charles E. Hummel* ≈

A few years ago, I had the idea to write a book called *To a Child LOVE Is Spelled T-I-M-E* and shared the idea with my friend, Lance Wubbels. Lance loved the concept and, about a week later, sent me an email with his story attached. He said, "How do you like this story as an introduction for the book?"

I can count on my hand the times in my life that I've been blown away by something I read. This was one of those times! This story bypassed my brain and went right to my soul. I immediately knew it was the perfect way to begin a book on this very important topic. I'm excited to share the introduction Lance wrote.

Introduction for
TO A CHILD LOVE IS SPELLED T-I-M-E

In the faint light of the attic, an old man, tall and stooped, bent his great frame and made his way to a stack of boxes that sat near one of the little half windows. Brushing aside a wisp of cobwebs, he tilted the top box toward the light and began to carefully lift out one old photograph album after another. Eyes once bright but now dim searched longingly for the source that had drawn him here.

It began with the fond recollection of the love of his life, long gone, and somewhere in these albums was a photo of her he hoped to rediscover. Silent as a mouse, he patiently opened the long-buried treasures and soon was lost in a sea of memories. Although his world had not stopped spinning when his wife left it, the past was more alive in his heart than his present aloneness.

Setting aside one of the dusty albums, he pulled from the box what appeared to be a journal from his grown son's childhood. He could not recall ever having seen it before or that his son had ever kept a journal. Why did Elizabeth always save the children's old junk? he wondered, shaking his white head.

Opening the yellowed pages, he glanced over a short reading, and his lips curved in an unconscious smile. Even his eyes brightened as he read the words that spoke clear and sweet to his soul. It was the voice of the little boy who had grown up far too fast in this very house and whose voice had grown fainter and fainter over the years. In the utter silence of the attic, the words of a guileless six-year-old worked their magic and carried the old man back to a time almost totally forgotten.

Entry after entry stirred a sentimental hunger in his heart like the longing a gardener feels in the winter for the fragrance of spring flowers. But it was accompanied by the painful memory that his son's simple recollections of those days were far different from his own. But how different?

Reminded that he had kept a daily journal of his business activities over the years, he closed his son's journal and turned to leave, having forgotten the cherished photo that originally triggered his search. Hunched over to keep from bumping his head on the rafters, the old man stepped to the wooden stairway and made his descent, then headed down a carpeted stairway that led to the den.

Opening a glass cabinet door, he reached in and pulled out an old business journal. Turning, he sat down at his desk and placed the two journals beside each other. His was leather-bound and engraved neatly with his name in gold, while his son's was tattered and the name "Jimmy" had been nearly scuffed from its surface. He ran a long, skinny finger over the letters, as though he could restore what had been worn away with time and use.

As he opened his journal, the old man's eyes fell upon an inscription that stood out because it was so brief in comparison to other days. In his own neat handwriting were these words:

"Wasted the whole day fishing with Jimmy. Didn't catch a thing."

With a deep sigh and a shaking hand, he took Jimmy's journal and found the boy's entry for the same day, June 4. Large, scrawling letters pressed deeply into the paper read:

"Went fishing with My Dad. Best day of My life."

Excerpted from the introduction of the Simple Truths book
To a Child LOVE Is Spelled T-I-M-E by Lance Wubbels

FAMILY

The greatest thing in family life is to take a hint when a hint
is intended—and not to take a hint when a hint isn't intended.

≈ *Robert Frost* ≈

The best and most beautiful things in the
world cannot be seen or even touched.
They must be FELT WITH THE HEART.

≈ *Helen Keller* ≈

The power of kindness

Too often, we underestimate the power of
a touch, a kind word, a listening ear, an honest
compliment, or the smallest act of caring,
all of which have the potential
to turn a life around.

≈ *Leo Buscaglia* ≈

There are some stories that, in their simplicity, are the most powerful. The following is one of those stories. Sometimes the smallest acts of kindness are those that change a lifetime.

PAID IN FULL

One day, a poor boy who was selling goods door-to-door to pay his way through school found he had only one thin dime left, and he was hungry. He decided he would ask for a meal at the next house. However, he lost his nerve when a lovely young woman opened the door.

Instead of a meal, he asked for a drink of water. She thought he looked hungry, so she brought him a large glass of milk. He drank it slowly, then asked, "How much do I owe you?"

"You don't owe me anything," she replied. "Mother has taught us never to accept pay for a kindness." He said, "Then I thank you from my heart."

As Howard Kelly left that house, he not only felt stronger physically, but his faith in God and man was strengthened also. He had been ready to give up and quit.

Years later, that young woman became critically ill. The local doctors were baffled. They finally sent her to the big city, where they called in specialists to study her rare disease.

Dr. Howard Kelly was called in for the consultation. When he heard the name of the town she came from, he walked down the hall of the hospital to her room. Dressed in his doctor's gown, he went in to see her and recognized her at once. He went back to the consultation room, determined to do his best to save her life. From that day, he gave special attention to the case.

After a long struggle, the battle was won. Dr. Kelly requested the business office pass the final bill to him for approval. He looked at it, wrote something on the edge, and sent it to her room. She feared to open it, for she was sure it would take the rest of her life to pay for it all. Finally, she looked and something caught her attention on the side of the bill. She read these words:

"Paid in full with one glass of milk..."
Dr. Howard Kelly

Dr. Howard Kelly was a distinguished physician who, in 1895, founded the Johns Hopkins Division of Gynecologic Oncology at Johns Hopkins University. According to Dr. Kelly's biographer, Audrey Davis, the doctor was on a walking trip through northern Pennsylvania one spring day when he stopped by a farmhouse for a drink of water.

Excerpted from the introduction of the Simple Truths book
The Secret to Living is Giving by Mac Anderson

KINDNESS

Kind words can be short and easy to speak,
but their echoes are truly endless.

≈ *Mother Teresa* ≈

Making a difference
with your life

WHAT YOU LEAVE BEHIND IS NOT WHAT IS
ENGRAVED IN STONE MONUMENTS, BUT WHAT
IS WOVEN INTO THE LIVES OF OTHERS.

≈ *Pericles* ≈

The letter hit my desk on June 10, 2003. I opened it to see a short, handwritten note attached to a single sheet of paper. The note was from Anna Lee Wilson, a Successories franchisee from Evansville, Indiana. "I know you have inspirational poems, and this is my all-time favorite. It's titled 'The Dash,' by Linda Ellis."

I can count on one hand how many times I've read something that stopped me in my tracks. This special poem is one that will stay in your mind—and in your heart—for years to come.

THE DASH

by Linda Ellis

I read of a man who stood to speak
at the funeral of a friend.
He referred to the dates on her tombstone
from the beginning…to the end.

He noted that first came the date of her birth
and spoke of the following date with tears,
but he said what mattered most of all
was the dash between those years.

For that dash represents all the time
that she spent alive on earth
and now only those who loved her
know what that little line is worth.

For it matters not, how much we own,
the cars…the house…the cash.
What matters is how we live and love
and how we spend our dash.

So think about this long and hard;
are there things you'd like to change?
For you never know how much time is left
that can still be rearranged.

If we could just slow down enough
to consider what's true and real
and always try to understand
the way other people feel.

(continued)

And be less quick to anger
and show appreciation more
and love the people in our lives
like we've never loved before.

If we treat each other with respect
and more often wear a smile…
remembering that this special dash
might only last a little while.

So when your eulogy is being read
with your life's actions to rehash,
would you be proud of the things they say
about how you spent your dash?

Excerpted from the introduction of the Simple Truths book
The Dash: Making a Difference with Your Life by Linda Ellis;
"The Dash" poem © 1996 Linda Ellis, www.Linda-Ellis.com

Love and kindness are
never wasted. They always

MAKE A DIFFERENCE.

They bless the one who receives them,
and they bless you, the giver.

≈ Barbara De Angelis ≈

What makes it all worthwhile

LOVE DOESN'T MAKE THE WORLD GO 'ROUND.
LOVE IS WHAT MAKES THE RIDE WORTHWHILE.

≈ Franklin P. Jones ≈

LOVE AND BE LOVED

A *story* by MAC ANDERSON

I had dinner with someone who told me that one of his best friends had been killed in a private plane crash. Something happened at the service that he'll never forget:

At the memorial service, his friend's wife walked to the podium to speak to the gathering. She said a friend had asked her the best memory she had of their life together. At the moment, she had been too grief-stricken to answer, but she thought about it since and wanted to answer the question.

They were in their late forties when he died, and she began talking about a time in their lives almost twenty years earlier. She had quit her job to obtain her master's degree, and her husband never wavered in his support.

He held down his own job and also did the cooking, cleaning, and other household chores while she studied for her degree.

One time, they both stayed up all night. She was finishing her thesis and he was preparing for an important business meeting. That morning, she walked out on their loft, looked at him over the railing, and just thought about how much she loved him. She knew how important this meeting was to his career, and she was feeling guilty that she didn't even have time to make his breakfast. He grabbed his briefcase and hurried out. She heard the garage door open and close, but much to her surprise, she heard it open again about thirty seconds later. From above, she watched her husband dash into the house and walk over to the neglected coffee table. Tracing his finger through the dust, he wrote the words "I love you." Then he raced back to his car.

The new widow then looked out at her audience and said, "John and I had a wonderful life together. We have been around the world several times; we've had everything money can buy…but nothing comes close to that moment."

Our lives move with lightning speed. It feels like yesterday that I graduated from college…and now forty years have passed. Although I'm very proud of my business accomplishments, in the end, my life comes back to loving and being loved.

Excerpted from the introduction of the Simple Truths book
 The Nature of Success by Mac Anderson

Unleashing the power of encouragement

YOU NEVER KNOW WHEN ONE KIND ACT, OR ONE WORD
OF ENCOURAGEMENT, CAN CHANGE A LIFE FOREVER.

≈ *Zig Ziglar* ≈

My friend David McNally's business failed when he was in his late twenties. He was in the depths of despair, convinced he would never rise to the top again. It was the candor and encouragement of his wife that helped him take control of his life again. He worked to build another successful business and is the author of several books, including one we coauthored, called *The Push*. In it, he shares a beautiful story about the power of encouragement. Enjoy!

THE PUSH

by David McNally

The eagle gently coaxed her offspring
toward the edge of the nest. Her heart quivered
with conflicting emotions as she felt their resistance
to her persistent nudging.

"Why does the thrill of soaring have to begin
with the fear of falling?" she thought. This ageless
question was still unanswered for her.

As in the tradition of the species, her nest was
located high upon the shelf of a sheer rock face.
Below there was nothing but air to support
the wings of each child.

"Is it possible that this time it will
not work?" she thought. Despite her fears
the eagle knew it was time. Her parental
mission was all but complete.

There remained one final task…the push.
The eagle drew courage from an innate wisdom.
Until her children discovered their wings, there was
   no purpose for their lives.

Until they learned how to soar, they would fail
to understand the privilege it was to have been born an eagle.
The push was the greatest gift she had to
   offer. It was her supreme act of love.

And so, one by one, she pushed them and…
   THEY FLEW.

Excerpted from the introduction of the Simple Truths book
The Push: Unleashing the Power of Encouragement by David McNally

It is *not* the mountain
WE CONQUER,
but ourselves.

≈ *Sir Edmund Hillary* ≈

The real meaning of success

❧

GOOD THINGS HAPPEN WHEN YOU
GET YOUR PRIORITIES STRAIGHT.

≈ *Scott Caan* ≈

PUT FIRST THINGS FIRST

A story by MAC ANDERSON

I met Charlie Cullen through his nephew during my sophomore year in college. Charlie was ranked by his peers as the top speaker in the country and had addressed the leaders of many Fortune 500 companies. But on this day, as a favor to his nephew, he interrupted his schedule to address a small group of students on the "Keys to Success." For almost an hour, he spoke passionately about courage, humility, perseverance, and believing in your dreams. And he ended with a story I never forgot.

He said he was in the Oklahoma City airport when he saw a woman walking along with three little girls. They were skipping and singing, "Daddy's coming home on a big jet! Daddy's coming home on a big jet!" All excited! Eyes lit up like diamonds! Wild anticipation! They had never before met Daddy coming home on a jet. Their mother was so proud of them and their enthusiasm. You could see it in her eyes.

43

Then the plane arrived, the door opened, and the passengers streamed in. You didn't have to ask which one was Daddy. The girls' bright eyes were glued on him. But his first look was for his wife. Spying her, he yelled, "Why didn't you bring my top coat?" and strode right past his adoring, crushed daughters.

You see…here was a man who had an opportunity to be great and he didn't recognize it.

How many times a day, a week, a month, a year, do we have the opportunity to be great, and not even know it?

Of all the beautiful lithographs that we created at Successories, everyone seems to remember one in particular. It is the photo of a small boy looking out at the ocean. The title is "Priorities," and it says, "A hundred years from now, it will not matter what my bank account was, the sort of house I lived in, or the kind of car I drove…but the world may be different because I was important in the life of a child."

These words truly bring the meaning of
"REAL SUCCESS" into focus.

Excerpted from the introduction of the Simple Truths book
The Nature of Success by Mac Anderson

I've learned that people will *forget* what you said,
people will *forget* what you did,
but people will *never forget*

HOW YOU MADE THEM FEEL.

≈ Maya Angelou ≈

A different mind-set

A TREE IS KNOWN BY ITS FRUIT; A MAN BY HIS DEEDS.
A GOOD DEED IS NEVER LOST; HE WHO SOWS
COURTESY REAPS FRIENDSHIP, AND HE WHO
PLANTS KINDNESS GATHERS LOVE.

≈ Saint Basil ≈

Sometimes, with all of the news stories we hear, we might think there really aren't very many good people in the world. But, as it turns out, kindness is always around us...if we are open to receiving it. You just need to hear a great story with a happy ending. Here's one of those stories.

KURTIS THE STOCK BOY *and* BRENDA THE CHECKOUT GIRL

In a supermarket, Kurtis the stock boy was busy working when a new voice came over the loud speaker asking for a carryout at register four. Kurtis was almost finished and wanted to get some fresh air so he decided to answer the call. As he approached the checkout stand, a distant smile caught his eye; the new checkout girl was beautiful.

Later that day, after his shift was over, he waited by the punch clock to find out her name. She came into the break room, smiled softly at him, took her card, punched out, and left. He looked at her card. BRENDA. He walked out only to see her start walking up the road. The next day, he waited outside as she left the supermarket and offered her a ride home. He looked harmless enough and she accepted. When he dropped her off, he asked if maybe he could see her again, outside of work. She simply said it wasn't possible.

He pressed and she explained that she had two children and couldn't afford a babysitter, so he offered to pay for one. Reluctantly, she accepted his offer for a date the following Saturday. That Saturday night, he arrived at her door only to have her tell him she was unable to go with him. The babysitter had called and canceled, to which Kurtis simply said, "Well, let's take the kids with us."

She tried to explain that taking the children was not an option, but again, not taking no for an answer, he pressed. Finally, Brenda brought him inside to meet her children. She had an older daughter who was just as cute as a bug, Kurtis thought. Then Brenda brought out her son, in a wheelchair. He was born a paraplegic with Down syndrome.

Kurtis asked Brenda, "I still don't understand why the kids can't come with us?" Brenda was amazed. Most men would run away from a woman with two kids, especially if one had disabilities—just like her first husband, the father of her children, had done. Kurtis was not ordinary; he had a different mind-set.

That evening, Kurtis and Brenda loaded up the kids and went to dinner and the movies. When her son needed anything, Kurtis would take care of him. When he needed to use the restroom, Kurtis picked him up out of his wheelchair, took him, and brought him back. The kids loved Kurtis. At the end of the evening, Brenda knew this was the man she was going to marry and spend the rest of her life with.

A year later, they were married and Kurtis adopted both of her children. Since then, they have added two more.

So what happened to Kurtis the stock boy and Brenda the checkout girl? Well, Mr. and Mrs. Kurt Warner now live in Arizona. He is the former quarterback of the Arizona Cardinals.

Is this a surprise ending, or could you have guessed that Kurt was not an ordinary person? Kurt was also the quarterback for the St. Louis Rams in Super Bowl XXXVI, where he was named Most Valuable Player. He was named the National Football League's Most Valuable Player twice.

I love great stories with HAPPY endings!

Excerpted from the introduction of the Simple Truths book
The Power of Kindness by Mac Anderson

CELEBRATE

the happiness that friends are always giving,
make every day a holiday and celebrate just living!

≈ *Amanda Bradley* ≈

Make your
time count

ENJOY THE LITTLE THINGS, FOR ONE DAY
YOU MAY LOOK BACK AND REALIZE THEY
WERE THE BIG THINGS.

≈ *Robert Brault* ≈

Time becomes even more precious as the years slip away. One of our customers sent me this story. Once you read it, you'll look at each Saturday (and every day) differently. See you at the toy store!

3,900 SATURDAYS

A story by JEFF DAVIS

The older I get, the more I enjoy Saturday morning. Perhaps it's the quiet solitude that comes with being the first to rise, or maybe it's the unbounded joy of not having to be at work. Either way, the first few hours of a Saturday morning are most enjoyable.

A few weeks ago, I was shuffling toward the garage with a steaming cup of coffee in one hand and the morning paper in the other. What began as a typical Saturday morning turned into one of those lessons that life seems to hand you from time to time. Let me tell you about it:

I turned the dial up on my ham radio and came across an older-sounding chap with a tremendous signal and a golden voice. You know the kind: he sounded like he should be in the broadcasting business. He was telling whomever he was talking with something about "a thousand marbles." I was intrigued and stopped to listen to what he had to say.

"Well, Tom, it sure sounds like you're busy with your job. I'm sure they pay you well, but it's a shame you have to be away from home and your family so much. Hard to believe a young fellow should have to work sixty or seventy hours a week to make ends meet. It's too bad you missed your daughter's dance recital," he continued. "Let me tell you something that has helped me keep my own priorities." And that's when he began to explain his theory of "a thousand marbles."

"You see, I sat down one day and did a little arithmetic. The average person lives about seventy-five years. I know, some live more and some live less, but on average, folks live about seventy-five years.

"Now then, I multiplied seventy-five times fifty-two and I came up with 3,900, which is the number of Saturdays that the average person has in their entire lifetime. Now, stick with me, Tom; I'm getting to the important part.

"It took me until I was fifty-five years old to think about all this in any detail," he went on, "and by that time, I had lived through more than 2,800 Saturdays. I got to thinking that if I lived to be seventy-five, I only had about a thousand of them left to enjoy. So I went to a toy store and bought every single marble they had. I ended up having to visit three toy stores to round up 1,000 marbles. I took them home and put them inside a large, clear plastic container right here in the shack next to my gear.

"Every Saturday since then, I have taken one marble out and thrown it away. I found that by watching the marbles diminish, I focused more on the really important things in life.

"There's nothing like watching your time here on this Earth run out to help get your priorities straight.

"Now let me tell you one last thing before I sign off with you and take my lovely wife out for breakfast. This morning, I took the very last marble out of the container. I figure that if I make it until next Saturday, I have been given a little extra time. And, the one thing we can all use is a little more time.

"It was nice to meet you, Tom. I hope you spend more time with your family, and I hope to meet you again here on the band. This is a seventy-five-year-old man, clear and good morning!"

You could have heard a pin drop on the band when this fellow signed off. I guess he gave us all a lot to think about. I had planned to work on the antenna that morning, and then I was going to meet up with a few hams to work on the next club newsletter.

Instead, I went upstairs and woke my wife with a kiss. "C'mon honey, I'm taking you and the kids to breakfast."

"What brought this on?" she asked with a smile.

"Oh, nothing special. It's just been a long time since we spent a Saturday together with the kids. And hey, can we stop at a toy store while we're out? I need to buy some marbles."

Excerpted from the introduction of the Simple Truths book
Charging the Human Battery: 50 Ways to Motivate Yourself by Mac Anderson

"Time is free, but

IT'S PRICELESS.

You can't own it, but you can use it.
You can't keep it, but you can spend it.
Once you've lost it you can
never get it back."

≈ *Harvey Mackay* ≈

Go the distance

BELIEVE AND ACT AS IF IT
WERE IMPOSSIBLE TO FAIL.

≈ *Charles F. Kettering* ≈

Many of us achieve success in one area of our lives, whether it's in our business, personal relationships, or our commitment to our communities. Despite tremendous personal challenges, this story of track star John Baker's commitment to "Finish Strong" shows the power of this philosophy both on and off the field. It's one that will remind you to go the distance to fulfill the really important things in life.

WHAT'S IN A NAME?

John Baker was too short and slight to be a runner for his high school track team. But John loved to run and he wanted to make the team. His best friend, John Haaland, was a tall and promising runner who was heavily recruited by the Manzano High School track coach, but he wanted nothing to do with the sport. John Baker convinced the track coach to let him join the team under the premise that his best friend would follow. The coach agreed, and John Baker became a runner.

The team's first meet was a 1.7-mile cross-country race through the foothills of Albuquerque. The reigning state champion, Lloyd Goff, was running, and all eyes were on him. The race began, and the pack of runners led by Goff disappeared behind the hill. The spectators waited. A minute passed, then two, and three. Then, the silhouette of a single runner appeared. The crowd assumed it was one of the favorites, but to everyone's amazement, it was John Baker leading the way to the finish line. In his first meet, he blew away the field and set a new meet record.

When asked what happened behind the hill, Baker explained that during the halfway point of the run, he was struggling hard. He asked himself a question: "Am I doing my best?" Still unsure if he truly was giving his best effort, he fixed his eyes on the back of the runner in front of him. "One at a time," he thought.

His entire focus was on one thing—to pass the runner in front of him. He committed to himself that nothing would distract him—fatigue, pain, nothing. One by one, he caught and passed each runner in front of him until there was no one else to pass.

As the season progressed, John proved that first race was not a fluke. Once the race began, the fun-loving, unassuming teenager became a fierce and relentless competitor who refused to lose. By the end of his junior year, John had broken six meet records and was largely regarded to be the best miler in the state. In his senior year, he ran the entire track and cross-country season undefeated, winning the state championship in both events. The future certainly looked bright for the seventeen-year-old.

John entered the University of New Mexico in 1962 and took his training to the next level by running more than ten miles a day. In the spring of 1965, Baker and his team faced the most feared team in track—the University of Southern California Trojans. There was little doubt that the mile belonged to the Trojans. During the race, Baker led for the first lap, then purposely slipped back to fourth. At the far turn of the third lap, Baker collided with another runner vying for position. Baker stumbled and struggled to stay on his feet, losing valuable time. With just under

330 yards to go, Baker dug deep, and living up to his reputation, he blew past the leaders to take the victory by three seconds.

Yes, the future looked even brighter for John Baker. After graduating college, Baker set his sights on the 1972 Olympics. In order to have time to train and also make a living, John took a coaching position at Aspen Elementary in Albuquerque where he had the opportunity to work with kids, something he always wanted to do. Within a few months, Coach Baker became known as the coach who cared. He invested a great deal of time and energy into working with his students as individuals. He was not a critical coach; he only demanded what he demanded of himself—that each child give his or her best effort. The kids responded and loved learning from Coach Baker.

In May 1969, just before his twenty-fifth birthday, John noticed that he was tiring prematurely from his workouts. Two weeks later, he developed chest pains, and one morning, he woke with a painfully swollen groin. He went to see his doctor, and they discovered that John had an advanced form of testicular cancer. The only chance John had was to undergo surgery. The operation confirmed the worst case; John's cancer had spread. His doctor believed he had at best six months to live. A second operation would be required.

John was devastated. How easy it would have been to lie down, quit, and feel sorry for himself. In fact, shortly before the second operation, John drove to the mountains and prepared to end his life. He did not want to put his family through the pain. Just before he thought of driving off the cliff, he recalled the faces of his children at Aspen and wondered if they would think this was the best that Coach Baker could do. This was not the legacy he wanted to leave behind.

At that moment, he decided to rededicate his life to his kids and continue striving to give his best effort. John was not a quitter. He drove home determined to give his best effort for the rest of his life.

In September, after extensive surgery and a summer of treatments, John returned to Aspen, where he added a unique program to include handicapped kids within the sports program. He appointed kids as "Coach's Time Keeper" or "Chief Equipment Supervisor." Everyone who wanted to participate was included. By Thanksgiving, letters from parents were arriving daily at Aspen Elementary in praise of Coach Baker. John created a special award for any child he thought deserved recognition. He used his own trophies as awards, carefully polishing off his own name. He purchased special fabric with his own money and at night would cut blue ribbons to give as awards.

John refused to take medication to help with his pain because he was afraid of how it would impair his ability to work with his kids. In early 1970, John was asked to help coach a small Albuquerque track club for girls, the Duke City Dashers. By that summer, the Dashers were a team to contend with. Baker boldly predicted that they would make it to the Amateur Athletic Union (AAU) finals.

By this time, Baker's condition was complicated by chemotherapy treatments. He could not keep any food down, his health rapidly deteriorated, and he struggled to make it to his practices. One October at practice, a girl ran up to Coach Baker and shouted, "Coach, your prediction came true. We're going to the AAU championship next month!" Baker was elated and wished for one remaining hope—to live long enough to go along. Unfortunately, it was not to be. A few weeks later, John clutched his abdomen and collapsed. He would not be able to make the trip. Then, at the age of twenty-six, on Thanksgiving Day in 1970, John Baker passed away, eighteen months after his first visit to the doctor. He had beaten the odds by twelve months. Two days later, the Duke City Dashers won the AAU championship in St. Louis—"for Coach Baker."

That would have been the end of the story, except a few days after his funeral, the children at Aspen Elementary began calling their school "John Baker School" and others rapidly adopted this change. A movement began to make the new name official. The Aspen principal referred the matter to the Albuquerque school board. In the spring of 1971, 520 families in the Aspen district voted on the matter. There were 520 votes for the name change and none against. That May, at a ceremony attended by hundreds of Baker's friends, family, and kids, Aspen Elementary officially became John Baker Elementary.

Today, John Baker Elementary stands as a testament to a courageous young man who believed in giving his best effort right down to the very end. His legacy continues through the dedicated efforts of the John Baker Foundation. The following poem was written by John five years before he was diagnosed with cancer:

Many thoughts race through my mind
As I step up to the starting line.
Butterflies thru my stomach fly
And as I free that last deep sigh,
I feel that death is drawing near,
But the end of the race I do not fear.
For when the string comes across my breast,
I know it's time for eternal rest.

The gun goes off, the race is run,
And only God knows if I've won.
My family and friends and many more
Can't understand what it was for.
But the "Race to Death" is a final test,
And I'm not afraid, for I've done my best.

—John Baker

Excerpted from the introduction of the Simple Truths book
Finish Strong: Amazing Stories of Courage and Inspiration by Dan Green

Warm your heart

TO GIVE WITHOUT ANY REWARD, OR ANY NOTICE,
HAS A SPECIAL QUALITY OF ITS OWN.

≈ *Anne Morrow Lindbergh* ≈

Our children can sometimes become our best teachers. While this story, by an unknown author, is about ice cream, it's guaranteed to warm your heart.

ICE CREAM FOR THE SOUL

Last week, I took my children to a restaurant. My six-year-old son asked if he could say grace. As we bowed our heads, he said, "God is good, God is great. Thank you for the food, and I would even thank you more if Mom gets us ice cream for dessert. And liberty and justice for all! Amen!"

Along with the laughter from the other customers nearby, I heard a woman remark, "That's what's wrong with this country. Kids today don't even know how to pray. Asking God for ice cream! Why, I never!"

Hearing this, my son burst into tears and asked me, "Did I do it wrong? Is God mad at me?"

As I held him, assuring him that he had done a terrific job and telling him God was certainly not mad at him, an elderly gentleman approached the table.

He winked at my son and said, "I happen to know that God thought that was a great prayer."

"Really?" my son asked.

"Cross my heart," the man replied.

Then, in a theatrical whisper, he added (indicating the woman whose remark had started this whole thing), "Too bad she never asks God for ice cream. A little ice cream is good for the soul sometimes."

Naturally, I bought my kids ice cream at the end of the meal. My son stared at his for a moment and then did something I will remember for the rest of my life.

He picked up his sundae and, without a word, walked over and placed it in front of the woman. With a big smile, he told her, "Here, this is for you. Ice cream is good for the soul sometimes, and my soul is good already."

Sometimes we all need some ICE CREAM.

Excerpted from the introduction of the Simple Truths book
The Power of Kindness by Mac Anderson

Say "thank you" today

❧

BE KIND AND MERCIFUL. LET NO ONE EVER COME TO
YOU WITHOUT COMING AWAY BETTER AND HAPPIER.

≈ *Mother Teresa* ≈

How many times have you actually thanked someone whose extra effort transformed your day...or your life? This story shows how much a simple gesture of appreciation can mean in someone's life.

THE LIFE-CHANGING
GIFT OF APPRECIATION

A story by BARBARA GLANZ

In my keynote speeches and workshops, CARE is an acronym I use for
the elements of a caring, creative, joyful (and more productive!) workplace and
home. The "A" in CARE stands for "Appreciation for ALL." As I speak about
appreciation, I use one of my favorite quotations from Albert Schweitzer:

"Sometimes our light goes out but is blown again into flame by an encounter
with another human being. Each of us owes the deepest thanks to those who
have rekindled this inner light."

Then I ask my audiences to please shut their eyes and think about someone
who at some time in their lives has rekindled their inner light. I leave the room in
silence for several minutes, and it is always a profound experience for everyone as
they remember the joy they received from being appreciated by someone when
they needed it the most.

Afterward, I ask them to write down the name of the person they thought
of and to commit to their own act of appreciation by letting that person know
in the next seventy-two hours that he or she was thought of. I suggest a phone

call, a note, or even a little prayer if they are no longer living.

After one moving session, a gentleman came up to talk with me and thanked me for creating a new awareness in him. He said he thought of his eighth-grade literature teacher because she was everyone's favorite teacher and had really made a difference in all of their lives. He planned to track her down and let me know what happened.

One afternoon, I received a call from him. He was choked up on the phone and could hardly get through his story. He said that it had taken him nearly two months to track his teacher down, and when he finally found her, he wrote to her.

The following week he received this letter:

Dear John,

You will never know how much your letter meant to me. I am eighty-three years old, and I am living all alone in one room. My friends are all gone. My family's gone. I taught fifty years and yours is the first "thank you" letter I have ever gotten from a student. Sometimes I wonder what I did with my life. I will read and reread your letter until the day I die.

He just sobbed on the phone. He said, "She is always the one we talk about at every reunion. She was everyone's favorite teacher—we loved her!" But no one had ever told her…until she received his letter.

Excerpted from the introduction of the Simple Truths book
The Simple Truths of Appreciation by Barbara Glanz

To the loved, a word of
affection is a morsel,
but to the loved-starved, a

WORD OF AFFECTION
can be a feast.

≈ *Max Lucado* ≈

Sportsmanship
at its best

❧

YOU GOTTA LOSE 'EM SOMETIMES.
WHEN YOU DO, LOSE 'EM RIGHT.

≈ *Casey Stengel* ≈

"It was the right thing to do." That's a phrase that struck me when I first heard the story of Sara Tucholsky. She was a college softball player who showed the world that the game is not always about winning and losing; it's about character, integrity, and sportsmanship.

RESPECT
WILL CARRY YOU HOME

Western Oregon University's Sara Tucholsky had no idea that the first— and, as it turns out, only—home run of her career would cause ripples that would make her last swing of the bat, as a college softball player, a national media sensation.

With two runners on and her team down a run to Central Washington University, Sara hit a home run to center field. As she rounded first base, she missed the bag. When she turned to tag the base, she injured her knee. Able only to crawl back to the base, Sara was told she would be called out if her teammates came to her aid. If a pinch runner checked into the game, her home run would count only as a single.

Players and fans alike were stunned when Central Washington first baseman Mallory Holtman, the conference's all-time home run leader, asked the umpire if there was any rule against opponents helping an injured player around the bases.

She was told there was not. Together, Holtman and short-stop Liz Wallace picked up Tucholsky and carried her around the bases, stopping at each bag to allow Sara to touch it with her good leg.

"It was the right thing to do," Holtman said in an interview on national television after the respectful act of sportsmanship had been witnessed by millions on ESPN and had become an Internet sensation.

The three runs sent Western Oregon to a 4–2 victory, ending Central Washington's chances of winning the conference and advancing to the playoffs.

"It's a great story," Western Oregon coach Pam Knox said, "something I'll never forget—the game's about character and integrity and sportsmanship, and it's not always about winning and losing."

As it turns out, the players who helped Sara had no idea of the circumstances surrounding the at-bat or that the story would make headlines around the country. "We didn't know that she was a senior or that this was her first home run," Wallace said Wednesday. "That makes the story more touching than it was. We just wanted to help her."

The gesture left Sara's Western Oregon teammates in tears. "I hope I would do the same for her in the same situation," Sara said. Central Washington coach Gary Frederick called the act of sportsmanship "unbelievable."

"In the end, it is not about winning and losing so much," Holtman, who initiated the act, said. "It was about this girl. She hit it over the fence and was in pain, and she deserved a home run."

Excerpted from the introduction of the Simple Truths book
Finish Strong Teen Athlete: A Guide for Developing the Champion Within by Dan Green

I'm not concerned with your liking
or disliking me. All I ask is that you
RESPECT ME
as a human being.

≈ Jackie Robinson ≈

A little kindness goes a long way

THOSE WHO BRING SUNSHINE INTO
THE LIVES OF OTHERS CANNOT KEEP
IT FROM THEMSELVES.

≈ *James M. Barrie* ≈

Opportunities abound every day to give to others. You just need to be ready to act on them—to make someone's day—and in doing so, to change someone's life. A story from *Random Acts of Kindness* is one that knocks the concept out of the park.

Make Someone's Day

by THE EDITORS OF CONARI PRESS

When I was in college, I worked part-time at a sporting goods store. There was a kid who would come by two or three times a week to visit this baseball mitt he wanted to buy. My manager and I would joke about him, not only because he was so dedicated and persistent, but also because he had picked the best and most expensive mitt in the store to obsess over.

This went on for months. The kid would come in, and you could tell he was so relieved that the mitt was still there. He would put it on, pound his fist into the pocket a couple of times, and then very carefully put it back on the shelf and leave.

Finally, one day, he came in with a shoe box and a smile about eight miles wide and announced that he wanted to buy the mitt. So the manager brought the mitt over to the cash register while the kid counted out a shoebox worth of nickels, quarters, and dimes. His stash came to exactly $19.98. The mitt cost $79.98, not including tax. My manager looked at the price tag, and sure enough the number seven was a little smudged, enough that a desperately hopeful seven-year-old could imagine it to be a one. Then he looked at me, smiled, and very carefully recounted.

"Yep, exactly $19.98." Wrapping up the mitt, he gave it to the boy.

Excerpted with permission from *Random Acts of Kindness:
An Illustrated Celebration* by the editors of Conari Press

You make a living by WHAT YOU GET
but you make a life by WHAT YOU GIVE.

≈ *Anonymous* ≈

Persistence
wins the race

A STRONG WILL, A SETTLED PURPOSE, AN INVINCIBLE
DETERMINATION CAN ACCOMPLISH ALMOST ANYTHING;
AND IN THIS LIES THE DISTINCTION BETWEEN
GREAT MEN AND LITTLE MEN.

≈ Thomas Fuller ≈

The power of the human spirit should never be underestimated. Read on to learn how persistence can change the world...at any age.

NEVER GIVE UP!

The year was 1983. In Australia, the long-distance foot race from Sydney to Melbourne was about to begin, covering 875 kilometers—more than 500 miles! About 150 world-class athletes had entered for what was planned as a six-day event, so race officials were startled when a sixty-one-year-old man approached and handed them his entry form.

His name was Cliff Young, and his "racing attire" included overalls and galoshes over his work boots.

At first, they refused to let him enter. He explained that he'd grown up on a 2,000-acre farm, with thousands of sheep. His family could afford neither horses nor tractors, so, when the storms came, his job was to round up the sheep. Sometimes, he said, it would take two or three days of running.

Finally, they let Cliff enter, and the race began. The others quickly left him way behind, shuffling along in his galoshes. But he didn't know the plan included stopping each night to rest, so he kept going.

By the fifth day, he had caught them all, won the race, and become a national hero. He continued to compete in long-distance races until he was in his seventies. He was an inspiration to millions and a great encourager of younger runners.

In 2004, the year after his death at age eighty-one, the organizers of the race where he first gained fame permanently changed its name to the Cliff Young Australian Six-Day Race in his honor and memory.

Excerpted from the Simple Truths book
The Best of Success: A Treasury of Inspiration by Bob Kelly

Do your work with your whole

HEART,

and you will succeed—
there's so little competition.

≈ *Elbert Hubbard* ≈

True leadership and caring

❁

NOBODY CARES HOW MUCH YOU KNOW,
UNTIL THEY KNOW HOW MUCH YOU CARE.

≈ *Theodore Roosevelt* ≈

WALK A MILE IN THEIR SHOES

A *story by* MAC ANDERSON

On March 5, 2003, I turned on **Good Morning America** *while eating* breakfast. Charlie Gibson was interviewing General Earl Hailston, the commanding general of Marine Forces Central Command. The general was waiting with his troops just a few miles off the border of Iraq…waiting to go to war. As he spoke, I was impressed by his humble and caring attitude.

Toward the end of the interview, his answer to a question touched me deeply. When Charlie asked him if he had any hobbies outside his work, the general said, "Yes, I love photography, especially taking photos of my men." He shared that while he had been waiting the past few days, he would take photos of his men, and at night, he would email the photos with a brief note to their mothers back in the United States. Charlie asked if he could see a sample of a letter, and the general walked into his tent and turned on his computer:

Dear Mrs. Johnson,

I thought you might enjoy seeing this picture of your son. He is doing great. I also wanted you to know that you did a wonderful job of raising him. You must be very proud. I can certainly tell you that I'm honored to serve with him in the U.S. Marines.

General Earl Hailston

I watched Charles randomly interview a few of General Hailston's men. You could feel the love and respect they had for their leader. Teddy Roosevelt's quote, "They don't care how much you know until they know how much you care," applies to General Hailston. He's a man who truly understood what caring, kindness, and leadership are all about.

Excerpted from the Simple Truths book
The Essence of Leadership by Mac Anderson

LEADERSHIP

A leader is one who knows the way, goes the way, and shows the way.

≈ *John C. Maxwell* ≈

Others there are whose
hands have sunbeams in
them, so that their grasp

WARMS MY
HEART.

≈ Helen Keller ≈

Choose your attitude

❧

YOU HAVE WITHIN YOU,
RIGHT NOW, EVERYTHING YOU
NEED TO DEAL WITH WHATEVER
THE WORLD CAN THROW AT YOU.

≈ *Brian Tracy* ≈

Author and poet BJ Gallagher has a way of capturing the emotions each of us feels while giving us a fresh perspective that can help "clear out the cobwebs." No matter what's happening in your life right now, BJ's poem "Weather Report" is just what you need to change your mood from stormy to sunny.

WEATHER REPORT

by BJ Gallagher

"Any day I'm vertical
is a good day"
…that's what I always say.
And I give thanks for my health.

If you ask me,
"How are you?"

I'll answer, "GREAT!"
because in saying so,
I make it so.
And I give thanks
I can choose my attitude.

When Life gives me dark clouds and rain,
I appreciate the moisture
that brings a soft curl to my hair.

When Life gives me sunshine,
I gratefully turn my face up
to feel its warmth on my cheeks.

When Life brings fog,
I hug my sweater around me
and give thanks for the cool shroud of mystery
that makes the familiar seem different
    and intriguing.

When Life brings snow,
I dash outside to catch the first flakes on
    my tongue,
relishing the icy miracle that is a snowflake.

Life's events and experiences
are like the weather—
they come and go,
no matter what my preference.

So, what the heck?!
I might as well decide to enjoy them.

For indeed,
there IS a time for every purpose
under Heaven.

And each season brings its own unique blessings…
and I give thanks.

Excerpted from the Simple Truths book
Learning to Dance in the Rain: The Power of Gratitude by BJ Gallagher

It took me a
long time

NOT TO

JUDGE MYSELF

through someone
else's eyes.

≈ *Sally Field* ≈

Believe with all your heart

FAITH CONSISTS IN BELIEVING
WHEN IT IS BEYOND THE POWER
OF REASON TO BELIEVE.

≈ *Voltaire* ≈

People can accomplish more than they think they can, if they dig deep and believe in themselves. In her book *The Best Things in Life Aren't Things*, author Peggy Anderson shares an example.

BREAKING THE FOUR-MINUTE MILE

*For more than one hundred years, runners tried to break the four-*minute mile. It was considered the "Holy Grail" of track and field. Many said it couldn't be done. In fact, doctors wrote articles in medical journals explaining why it was physically impossible for the human body to run a mile in less than four minutes.

However, in May 1954, a British medical student named Roger Bannister ran the mile in 3:59.4. His amazing accomplishment made headlines around the world. Yet, what happened afterward is even more amazing. The four-minute mile was broken again the next month...and then again...and again. It has since been broken more than seven hundred times, sometimes by several people in the same race.

What happened? They weren't training any differently, but for the first time, they believed they could do it. The barriers to the mind had come down.

Never underestimate the power of belief when it comes to fulfilling your dreams. I can say with no hesitation that every person I've ever met who has achieved any degree of success has had one thing in common: they believed with all their heart they could do it.

Whether you think you can or think you can't,
YOU'RE RIGHT!
≈ *Henry Ford* ≈

Excerpted from the Simple Truths book
The Best Things in Life Aren't Things:
10 Essentials for a Meaningful Life by Peggy Anderson

Love is enough
to get you through

❧

MY FATHER GAVE ME THE GREATEST GIFT
ANYONE COULD GIVE ANOTHER PERSON,
HE BELIEVED IN ME.

≈ *Jim Valvano* ≈

The Olympics often provide stories you remember for years after the event. In this special story, the gold medal goes to love and courage...

A FATHER'S LOVE

In August 1992, Derrick Redmond from Great Britain was favored to win the 400-meter race during the summer Olympic Games in Barcelona, Spain, but as he powered around the backstretch, his hamstring snapped. Derrick tried desperately to finish the race, but he still had half the distance to go. Because he couldn't walk, he began to hop. One step—a grimace. Two steps—a yell.

Jim Redmond had to get to his struggling son. He doesn't remember all the steps down from Section 131, Row 22, Seat 25 of the Olympic Stadium. He doesn't really remember leaping over the railing or pushing off security guards who were too stunned to stop him. He was not just a spectator at the Olympics anymore; Jim Redmond was a father, and he had to get to his son.

"Dad," Derrick said. "Dad… Get me back to lane five. I want to finish."

Leaning on each other, father and son made their way around the track as the crowd, with the whole world watching, rose to their feet, cheering. Olympic organizers can light the skies with fireworks, they can invite kings and queens…but this was the magic of real life.

That day, people saw an example of great courage, but they witnessed an even greater story about love.

Love, simply stated, is the essence of life. It can put the smile on your face, the bounce in your step, and, most importantly, the joy in your heart. Even when your whole world is crumbling around you, one person holding your hand, looking into your eyes, saying "I love you" is enough to get you through.

A POEM *by* Robert A. Ward

I wish you the courage to be warm when the world
　　Would prefer that you be cool.
　　I wish you success sufficient to your needs;
　　I wish you failure to temper that success.
I wish you joy in all your days; I wish you sadness
　　So that you may better measure that joy.
I wish you gladness to overbalance grief.
I wish you humor and a twinkle in the eye.
I wish you glory and the strength to bear its burdens.
I wish you sunshine on your path and storms to season
　　Your journey.
I wish you peace in the world in which you live and in the
　　Smallest corner of the heart where truth is kept.
I wish you faith to help define your living and your life.
More I cannot wish you, except perhaps love, to make
　　All the rest worthwhile.

Excerpted from the Simple Truths book
The Power of Attitude by Mac Anderson

The true meaning of love

NEVER BELIEVE THAT A FEW CARING PEOPLE
CAN'T CHANGE THE WORLD. FOR, INDEED,
THAT'S ALL WHO EVER HAVE.

≈ *Margaret Mead* ≈

This is a wonderful story. I don't know who wrote it, but it captures the essence of caring, kindness, and love.

SOMEONE WHO CARES

It was a busy morning, approximately 8:30 a.m., when an elderly gentleman in his eighties arrived to have stitches removed from his thumb. He said he was in a hurry since he had an appointment at 9:00 a.m.

I took his vital signs and had him take a seat, knowing it would be more than an hour before someone would be able to see him. I saw him looking at his watch and decided since I was not busy with another patient, I would evaluate his wound.

On exam, it was well healed, so I talked to one of the doctors, got the needed supplies to remove his sutures, and redressed his wound. We began to talk and I asked him if he had a doctor's appointment since he was in such a hurry. The gentleman told me no, that he needed to go to the nursing home to eat breakfast with his wife.

I asked about her health. He told me she had been at the nursing home for a while and that she was a victim of Alzheimer's disease. As we talked and I finished dressing his wound, I asked if she would be worried if he was a bit late. He replied that she no longer knew who he was—that she had not recognized him in five years.

I was surprised and asked him, "And you still go every morning, even though she doesn't know who you are?" He smiled as he patted my hand and said, "She doesn't know me, but I still know who she is."

I had to hold back tears as he left. I had goose bumps on my arm and thought, "That is the kind of love I want in my life." True love is neither physical nor romantic. True love is an acceptance of all that is, has been, will be, and will not be.

Excerpted from the Simple Truths book
The Power of Kindness by Mac Anderson

Life's key lesson

❧

WE HAVE COMMITTED THE
GOLDEN RULE TO MEMORY;
LET US NOW COMMIT IT TO LIFE.

≈ *Edwin Markham* ≈

REMEMBER RULE NO. 1...
IT'S GOLDEN

A story by MAC ANDERSON

I grew up in Trenton, a west Tennessee town of five thousand people. I have wonderful memories of those first eighteen years, and many people in Trenton influenced my life in very positive ways. My football coach, Walter Kilzer, taught me the importance of hard work, discipline, and believing in myself. My history teacher, Fred Culp, is still the funniest person I've ever met. He taught me that a sense of humor, and especially laughing at yourself, can be one of life's greatest blessings.

But my father was my hero. He taught me many things, but at the top of the list, he taught me to treat people with love and respect...to live the Golden Rule. I remember one particular instance of him teaching this "life lesson" as if it were yesterday. Dad owned a furniture store, and I used to dust the furniture every Wednesday after school to earn my allowance. One afternoon, I observed my dad talking to all the customers as they came in...a hardware store owner, a banker, a farmer, a doctor. At the end of the day, just as Dad was closing, the garbage collector came in.

I was ready to go home, and I thought that surely Dad wouldn't spend too much time with him. But I was wrong. Dad greeted him at the door with a big hug and talked with him about his wife and son who had been in a car accident the month before. He empathized, he asked questions, he listened, and he listened some more. I kept looking at the clock, and when the man finally left, I asked, "Dad, why did you spend so much time with him? He's just the garbage collector." Dad then looked at me, locked the front door to the store, and said, "Son, let's talk."

He said, "I'm your father, and I tell you lots of stuff as all fathers should, but if you remember nothing else I ever tell you, remember this…treat every human being just the way that you would want to be treated. I know this is not the first time you've heard it, but I want to make sure it's the first time you truly understand it, because if you had understood, you would never have said what you said."

We sat there and talked for another hour about the meaning and the power of the Golden Rule. Dad said, "If you live the Golden Rule, everything else in life will usually work itself out, but if you don't, your life probably will be very unhappy and without meaning."

I recently heard someone say, "If you teach your child the Golden Rule, you will have left them an estate of incalculable value." Truer words were never spoken.

Excerpted from the Simple Truths book
The Power of Attitude by Mac Anderson

COMPASSION

Resolve to be tender with the young, compassionate with the aged,

sympathetic with the striving, and tolerant with the weak…

sometime in your life you will have been all of these.

≈ *Dr. Robert H. Goddard* ≈

Learn how to live

THE BRICK WALLS ARE NOT THERE TO KEEP US OUT;
THE BRICK WALLS ARE THERE TO GIVE US A CHANCE
TO SHOW HOW BADLY WE WANT SOMETHING.

≈ *Randy Pausch* ≈

THE ELEPHANT IN THE ROOM

Randy Pausch was forty-seven years old when he died from pancreatic cancer. He was, as *The Independent of London* put it, "the dying man who taught America how to live." His book *The Last Lecture* is an international bestseller and offers many wonderful lessons about life.

Randy Pausch's "last lecture" was delivered in September 2007 at Carnegie Mellon University, where he taught computer science. The lecture began with him standing before a screen beaming down chilling CT images of tumors in his liver, under the title "The Elephant in the Room."

"I have about six months to live," he said to a stunned audience. "I'm really in good shape, probably better shape than most of you," then dropped to the floor to do push-ups.

He went on to say, "I'm dying and I'm having fun, and I'm going to keep having fun every day I have left." He talked about his childhood dreams and what they had taught him about life. "If you live your life the right way, the karma will take care of itself…your dreams will come to you."

Randy Pausch really was a dying man who taught America how to live.

He died July 25, 2008, but his wisdom, his passion, and his attitude are lasting sources of inspiration for all of us.

Excerpted from the Simple Truths book
Charging the Human Battery: 50 Ways to Motivate Yourself
by Mac Anderson

Never lose the
CHILDLIKE WONDER...
Show gratitude... Don't complain;
just work harder... Never give up.

≈ Randy Pausch ≈

Put life into perspective

❧

LIFE MUST BE LIVED AS PLAY.

≈ *Plato* ≈

This poem by an unknown author puts life into perspective. It's a great reminder to not let life pass you by while you are waiting for something else.

A POEM *by* unknown

First I was dying to finish high school and start college.
And then I was dying to finish college and start working.
And then I was dying to marry and have children.
And then I was dying for my children
to grow old enough so I could go back to work.
And then I was dying to retire.
And now I am dying...
and suddenly realize that I forgot to live.

Excerpted from the Simple Truths book
Charging the Human Battery: 50 Ways to
Motivate Yourself by Mac Anderson

Belief fuels enthusiasm

NOTHING GREAT IN THE WORLD HAS EVER
BEEN ACCOMPLISHED WITHOUT PASSION.

≈ *Georg Wilhelm Friedrich Hegel* ≈

RIDE THE WAVE OF PASSION

A story by MAC ANDERSON

What happens when you believe something with all your heart? Belief fuels enthusiasm, and determined enthusiasm explodes into passion. It fires our souls and lifts our spirits.

In 1991, when Successories hired Tim Dumler as a corporate account manager, he shared his goal of becoming number one in the company with his manager, Neil Sexton. But Neil, quite frankly, had serious doubts that Tim could make it through the first month, much less be number one.

Neil's first two interviews with Tim were conducted over the phone, and he passed those with flying colors. But when Neil met Tim for the first time, he was shocked when Tim told him he was legally blind. He began to lose his sight when he was in the third grade from a disease called macular degeneration. Tim acknowledged he would have problems entering orders into the computers, but he had a possible solution. He told Neil about a machine he could hook up to magnify the letters on the screen to two inches high. Tim was willing to buy it if he could have the job.

After the conversation, Neil came to my office and explained the situation. I said, "Neil, let's give him a chance," but I must admit, I had serious doubts that Tim could do it.

Well, we were dead wrong. We grossly underestimated Tim's passion and his determination to succeed. Even though it took him much longer to enter the orders, Tim made it work. He came in early. He worked late. Whatever it took, he did it.

In 1991, Tim's first year, he was at the top of ten experienced corporate sales reps, with more than $500,000 in sales. In 1994, he was number one again with $700,000 and again in 1997 with $950,000. His customers loved him because when you can't see, you become a great listener. His peers loved him because of his caring, positive attitude.

He was certainly an inspiration to me, too. I asked him one time, "Tim, how do you stay so positive?" He said, "Mac, it's unfortunate that I'm visually impaired, but I have to tell you that fighting through the adversity has made me a better person. I have come to realize that I have a lot more than I don't have. I love my family, my work, and the people I work with. I've been blessed in many ways."

Tim's passion has propelled him to great successes.

Excerpted from the Simple Truths book
The Nature of Success by Mac Anderson

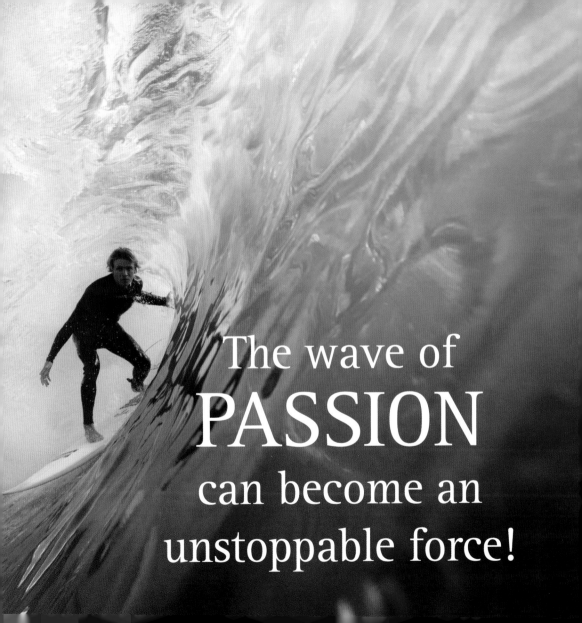

The wave of
PASSION
can become an
unstoppable force!

Touching the
next generation

❊

MOST OF US END UP WITH NO MORE THAN FIVE OR
SIX PEOPLE WHO REMEMBER US. TEACHERS HAVE
THOUSANDS OF PEOPLE WHO REMEMBER THEM
FOR THE REST OF THEIR LIVES.

≈ Andrew Rooney ≈

Teachers hold a special place in my heart as, I'm sure, they do in yours. Their dedication to the next generation makes a difference in the lives of their students...sometimes in ways that even they don't expect. This story is one I think you'll love.

THE STORY OF MARK EKLUND

by SISTER HELEN MROSLA

He was in the first third-grade class I taught at Saint Mary's School in Morris, Minnesota. All thirty-four of my students were dear to me, but Mark Eklund was one in a million. Very neat in appearance, he had that happy-to-be-alive attitude that made even his occasional mischievousness delightful.

Mark talked incessantly. I had to remind him again and again that talking without permission was not acceptable. What impressed me so much, though, was his sincere response every time I had to correct him for misbehaving. "Thank you for correcting me, Sister!" I didn't know what to make of it at first, but before long, I became accustomed to hearing it many times a day.

One morning, my patience was growing thin when Mark talked once too often, and then I made a novice teacher's mistake. I looked at Mark and said, "If you say one more word, I am going to tape your mouth shut!" It wasn't ten seconds later when Chuck blurted out, "Mark is talking again." I hadn't asked any of the students to help me watch Mark, but since I had stated the punishment in front of the class, I had to act on it. I remember the scene as if it had occurred this morning. I walked to my desk, very deliberately opened my drawer, and took out a roll of masking tape. Without saying a word, I proceeded to Mark's desk, tore off two pieces of tape, and made a big X with them over his mouth. I then returned to the front of the room. As I glanced at Mark to see how he was doing, he winked at me. That did it! I started laughing. The class cheered as I walked back to Mark's desk, removed the tape, and shrugged my shoulders. His first words were, "Thank you for correcting me, Sister."

At the end of the year, I was asked to teach junior high math. The years flew by, and before I knew it, Mark was in my classroom again and just as polite. Since he had to listen carefully to my instruction in the "new math," he did not talk as much in ninth grade as he had in third. One Friday, things just didn't feel right. We had worked hard on a new concept all week, and I sensed that the students were frustrated with themselves and edgy with one another. I had to stop this crankiness before it got out of hand. So I asked them to list the names of the other students in the room on two sheets of paper, leaving a space between each name. Then I told them to think of the nicest thing they  could say about each of their classmates and write it down. It took the remainder of the class period to finish their assignment, and as the students left the room, each one handed me the papers. Charlie smiled. Mark said, "Thank you for teaching me, Sister. Have a good weekend."

That Saturday, I wrote down the name of each student on a separate sheet of paper, and I listed what everyone else had said about that individual.

On Monday I gave each student his or her list. Before long, the entire class was smiling. "Really?" I heard whispered. "I never knew that meant anything to any-one!" "I didn't know others liked me so much." No one ever mentioned those papers in class again. I never knew if they discussed them after class or with their parents, but it didn't matter. The exercise had accomplished its purpose. The students were happy with themselves and one another again.

That group of students moved on. Several years later, after I returned from vacation, my parents met me at the airport. As we were driving home, Mother asked me the usual questions about the trip, the weather, and my experiences in general. There was a lull in the conversation. Mother gave Dad a sideways glance and simply said, "Dad?"

My father cleared his throat as he usually did before something important. "The Eklunds called last night," he began. "Really?" I said. "I haven't heard from them in years. I wonder how Mark is." Dad responded quietly. "Mark was killed in Vietnam. The funeral is tomorrow, and his parents would like it if you could attend." To this day, I can still point to the exact spot on I-494 where Dad told me about Mark.

I had never seen a serviceman in a military coffin before. Mark looked so handsome, so mature. All I could think at that moment was, "Mark, I would give all the masking tape in the world if only you would talk to me."

The church was packed with Mark's friends. Chuck's sister sang "The Battle Hymn of the Republic." Why did it have to rain on the day of the funeral? It was difficult enough at the graveside. The pastor said the usual prayers, and the bugler played "Taps." One by one, those who loved Mark took a last walk by the coffin and sprinkled it with holy water. I was the last one to bless the coffin. As I stood there, one of the soldiers who acted as pallbearer came up to me. "Were you Mark's math teacher?" he asked. I nodded as I continued to stare at the coffin. "Mark talked about you a lot," he said.

After the funeral, most of Mark's former classmates headed to Chuck's farmhouse for lunch. Mark's mother and father were there, obviously waiting for me. "We want to show you something," his father said, taking a wallet out of his pocket. "They found this on Mark when he was killed. We thought you might recognize it." Opening the billfold, he carefully removed two worn pieces of notebook paper that had obviously been taped, folded, and refolded many times. I knew without looking that the papers were the ones on which I had listed all the good things each of Mark's classmates had said about him.

"Thank you so much for doing that," Mark's mother said. "As you can see, Mark treasured it." Mark's classmates started to gather around us. Charlie smiled rather sheepishly and said, "I still have my list. I keep it in the top drawer of my desk at home." Chuck's wife said, "Chuck asked me to put his in our wedding album." "I have mine too," Marilyn said. "It's in my diary." Then Vicki, another classmate, reached into her pocketbook, took out her wallet, and showed her worn and frazzled list to the group. "I carry this with me at all times," Vicki said without batting an eyelash. "I think we all saved our lists." That's when I finally sat down and cried. I cried for Mark and for all his friends who would never see him again.

Excerpted from the Simple Truths book
The Heart of a Teacher: A Treasury of Inspiration
by Paula J. Fox

TO LIVE *by* unknown

"There once was a very cautious man,
Who never laughed or cried,
He never cared, he never dared,
He never dreamed or tried.
And when one day he passed away,
His insurance was denied.
For since he never really lived,
They claimed he never died."

Excerpted from the Simple Truths book
The Nature of Success by Mac Anderson

How to make your dreams come true

DISCOVER THE POWER OF DISCIPLINE

A story by MAC ANDERSON

Aristotle said, "We are what we repeatedly do. Excellence then is not an act but a habit." How true that is! If we make good habits, they invariably make us.

In the fall of 1996, I received a phone call from an unforgettable young man. He introduced himself as Matt Ghaffari and went on to tell me that, a few months earlier, he had won the silver medal in Greco-Roman wrestling during the 1996 Summer Olympics. He said he wanted to stop by while he was in Chicago, and I said, "No problem. I'd like to meet you."

A few hours later, my receptionist called saying my guest had arrived. I walked to the lobby and there he was…six-foot-four and 286 pounds of solid muscle. He had a huge smile on his face as we walked back to my office.

When we sat down, he said, "Mr. Anderson, I've come to thank you because you and your company have made a difference in my life." Then he reached into his left pocket and pulled out a green felt cloth, which he then opened. There it was, his silver medal. It was beautiful! Then he reached into his right pocket and emptied the contents onto my desk. Amid his change was one of the brass medallions that we had created at Successories with the words "Expect to Win."

He said, "Mr. Anderson, I've had that medallion in my pocket every day for three years. For the past four years, I've worked ten hours a day, six days a week to train my body to be an Olympic champion. But I knew the difference in winning and losing was not going to be training my body; it was going to be training my mind to think positive, powerful thoughts—to believe I could do it. And the products you've created at Successories have helped me to think like a champion."

You see, winners like Matt Ghaffari are never complacent. That is why they're winners. They understand the power of discipline. They understand one of my favorite laws in life—you cannot get what you've never had unless you're willing to do what you've never done.

Are you willing to make the sacrifices required to make your dreams come true?

Excerpted from the Simple Truths book
The Nature of Success by Mac Anderson

DISCIPLINE

The difference between a successful person and others
is not a lack of strength, not a lack of knowledge,
but rather a lack of will.

≈ *Vince Lombardi* ≈

CONCLUSION

I hope you found these stories as inspirational as I did.
When you are in need of an "attitude adjustment,"
just pick up this book again...or share it with a friend.

It's sure to give you "goose bumps" when you need them most.

MAC ANDERSON

Mac Anderson is the founder of Simple Truths and Successories, Inc., the leader in designing and marketing products for motivation and recognition. These companies, however, are not the first success stories for Mac. He was also the founder and CEO of McCord Travel, the largest travel company in the Midwest and part owner/vice president of sales and marketing for the Orval Kent Company, the country's largest manufacturer of prepared salads.

His accomplishments in these unrelated industries provide some insight into his passion and leadership skills. He also brings the same passion to his speaking, where he speaks to many corporate audiences on a variety of topics, including leadership, motivation, and team building.

For more information about Mac, visit www.simpletruths.com.

Mac has authored or coauthored twenty-four books that have sold more than four million copies.

- *The Best of Success*
- *Change is Good... You Go First*
- *Charging the Human Battery*
- *Customer Love*
- *The Dash*
- *The Essence of Leadership*
- *Even Eagles Need a Push*
- *Finding Joy*
- *Learning to Dance in the Rain*
- *Leadership Quotes*
- *212° Leadership*
- *212°: The Extra Degree*
- *212° Service*
- *Habits Die Hard*
- *Motivational Quotes*
- *The Nature of Success*
- *One Choice*
- *The Power of Attitude*
- *The Power of Kindness*
- *The Road to Happiness*
- *The Secret to Living Is Giving*
- *To a Child, Love Is Spelled T-I-M-E*
- *You Can't Send a Duck to Eagle School*
- *What's the Big Idea?*

If you have enjoyed this book, we invite you to check out
our entire collection of gift books, with free inspirational movies,
at **www.simpletruths.com.** You'll discover it's a great way to inspire
friends and family, or to thank your best customers and employees.

FOR MORE INFORMATION, PLEASE VISIT US AT:

WWW.SIMPLETRUTHS.COM
OR CALL TOLL FREE...800-900-3427